Anonymous

Ecclesiastical Reform

The present state of the clergy of the Established Church considered

Anonymous

Ecclesiastical Reform
The present state of the clergy of the Established Church considered

ISBN/EAN: 9783337260385

Printed in Europe, USA, Canada, Australia, Japan

Cover: Foto ©Lupo / pixelio.de

More available books at **www.hansebooks.com**

Ecclesiastical Reform.

THE PRESENT STATE OF THE CLERGY OF THE ESTABLISHED CHURCH, CONSIDERED.

IN THREE PARTS.

I. Of the various *abuses* occasioned by the conduct of our prelates.

II. Of the oppression of the *incumbents*, the pluralists, towards their substitutes.

III. Of the miserable state of the *curates*, whose salaries are so very disproportionate to the value of the benefices of their employers.

By A BENEFICED CLERGYMAN,
OF THE UNIVERSITY OF CAMBRIDGE.

LONDON:

PRINTED FOR E. WILLIAMS, BOOKSELLER, N° 13, STRAND; AND T. WILLIAMS, N° 156, LEADENHALL STREET.

M.DCC.XCII.

ECCLESIASTICAL REFORM.

PART THE FIRST.

Treats of the various ABUSES in the Eſtabliſhed Church, owing to the Conduct of the BISHOPS.

IT is univerſally acknowledged, that perſons miniſtring in things ſacred, have always been held in the higheſt veneration and reſpect; not only in civilized countries, but even among the moſt barbarous part of mankind, ſuch as officiate in their religious worſhips of whatever kind it be, are held in eſteem and reverence.

The ancient Romans, although pagans, conſidered it a peculiar honour to be elected into the high office of Pontifex; the moſt illuſtrious of the Roman ſenate aſpired to that dignity, eſteeming it the moſt honourable office of the ſtate. With reſpect to ſacred hiſtory, it appears from the Old Teſtament, that the

the priesthood was founded on terms the most honourable: when the first born and head of the family was appointed into that office; when the prince and the priest were united into one and the same person; and to have a right to minister in holy things, was esteemed, among the Jews, the highest degree of nobility.

We also find in the New Testament, that the gospel confers the highest titles and appellations of honour, upon such as devoted themselves to the service of the Deity. The great apostle of the Gentiles *commands them to be obeyed and esteemed very highly in love, for their works' sake.*

The apostolic age received them, even as *the angels of God*, gladly ministred to their necessities, were ready to do them every possible service, and shew them the highest respect. We find that converted kingdoms admitted them to the most important trusts; enacted edicts, settled revenues, and granted them peculiar privileges and immunities, protecting their persons

persons from violence, and shielding their reputation from slander and reproach.

In latter times, when this zeal and reverence began in some degree to abate, the laws of the church endeavoured to revive it: as we find it thus expressed in one of their capitulars; *ut omnes suis sacerdotibus, tam majoris ordinis, quam inferioris, a minimo usque ad maximum, ut summo Deo, cujus vice in ecclesia legatione funguntur, obedientes existant.*

The grounds upon which the scripture requires that the clergy in all ages should be held in such estimation and honour, is, the dignity and great majesty of the Master they serve; *let a man account of us*, says the apostle, *as of the ministers of Christ.*

In order to add the more weight, respect, and veneration to their office and ministration, particular care was observed in the Levitical law, that no person who had any blemish, or personal defect, should be admitted to the priesthood to minister in the service of the Deity.

For the same reason, strict caution is given to all Christian bishops, *that they lay not hands suddenly*

suddenly upon any one. This is also forbid by the canons of our church. But, how little are these prohibitions attended to by the Prelates of our church, who admit into the sacred office of the ministry, the most contemptible beings in personal appearance; the dregs and refuse of every other profession or occupation, of which I could point out a variety of instances, was it not an invidious task? Some of the military profession, who had been broke for cowardice and other misbehaviours; others, who, not succeeding in the profession of the law and physic; broken tradesmen also; who, by some of our bishops have been admitted into the church by ordination, without any previous study or preparation, to the no small disparagement of the ministerial function: have, by the solicitation of friends, or some other motives, been instantly put upon a level with gentlemen who have spent many years, as well as hundreds of pounds, in a regular university education, and had taken proper degrees to qualify themselves for the ministry.— Commissioning persons of the above description

tion to officiate in religious myſteries, is, a reflection upon the venerable order of our Prelates; a kind of profanation of things ſacred; an injuſtice to the regular bred univerſity gentlemen; a diſparagement to the profeſſion in general: in fine, it is a groſs affront to the Deity in *particular*, to ſuppoſe that the refuſe and dregs of every other occupation in life, are ſufficiently qualified for HIS SERVICE. Was there a deficiency of regular clergy for the ſupply of the miniſtry in the eſtabliſhed church, there might indeed be ſome excuſe for the conduct of our biſhops in this particular; but it is notorious, that there are a ſuperabundance of expectants, miſerably diſtreſſed, for want of appointments in the church, even of the moſt inconſiderable ſalary. What I have advanced, with regard to reſpect due to the clerical profeſſion, is not with a view of magnifying the office; but to ſhew the impropriety of our biſhops ordaining perſons of the above deſcription, to the diſparagement of the function, to officiate in the church, and to partake of its revenue, to the excluſion of ſuch

as

as have been regularly educated in our universities for that purpose, with an expectation of being maintained thereby, in recompense for the time and expence they had been at in qualifying themselves for the profession: this, by the dispassionate and judicious part of mankind, is esteemed a great grievance, as well as the height of injustice.

There is an abuse of great magnitude in our church, occasioned by the Archbishop of Canterbury; which is, his granting DISPENSATIONS to hold two benefices at a time. It is true the law, as it unfortunately stands at present, grants him this power, and peculiar privilege; but it is an evil, which remained uncorrected at the reformation; it was a prerogative which the pope usurped, and, since that time, has been continued to the metropolitan of our church. This, by multiplying pluralities, occasions non-residence, and consequently neglect of the cure of souls, which the incumbents had solemnly undertaken to attend to, as well as much inequality among the clergy: large incomes to *some*, and incompetent provision

vision and maintenances for *others*; which excites a contempt of their persons and administrations, in the opinion of the laity.

Considering the regard his Majesty has for the prosperity of the established church, I am pretty confident, was HE made sensible how greatly the happiness and respectability of the clergy would be advanced, and the cause of religion promoted, by with-holding his confirmation of the archbishop's faculties, there would be a speedy end to this monstrous abuse now prevailing in our church.

OPTION, another relic of popery unreformed. It is a peculiar privilege which the archbishop's claim as their prerogative in their respective provinces. When either of the Archbishops consecrate a suffragan bishop in their respective provinces, they constantly make choice of the most valuable piece of preferment in that diocese, and collate a favourite chaplain, or some friend they think proper into it, upon the death of the incumbent.

Permitting bishops to hold livings in COMMENDAM, is another scandalous abuse in the established

established church, totally different at present, from its original intention, which I shall explain.

COMMENDAMS then, were of very ancient and laudable institution, upon their *first origin*; for when an elective benefice, that was juspatronatus, for which the ordinary could not, for some reason, provide immediately, the care of it was recommended by the superior to some man of merit, who should take upon him the direction of it, *only* till the vacancy should be filled up, but could *enjoy none of the profits*: therefore some excellent person was generally pitched upon, to whom the undertaking was an expence, and had nothing to recommend it; but the trouble he was to undergo, was for the service of the church: such a person, then, would very improperly be said to hold this benefice in Commendam, as is practised amongst us at present; consequently, in reality, he could not be said to hold *two benefices*. First, the Commendam was to continue *only* till other provision was made; then, it grew to be for a determined time, *six months only*; thus, this abuse gained ground gradually, till

it

it arrived to the shameful height, and I may add, sacrilegious abuse now practised.

How can a spiritual governor of the church answer it to his conscience, when he holds one, sometimes two valuable benefices in *commendam*, with a bishoprick, the revenue of which is, *alone*, amply sufficient to keep up the dignity of his station?

NON-RESIDENCE another evil. The pretence of the bishops for absenting themselves the greater part of the year from their dioceses, is, their attendance in parliament.——I appeal to every considerate person, even to the prelates themselves, whether they do not in conscience suppose, that their attendance and residence in their respective dioceses, to regulate and superintend the affairs of their clergy; to have an eye upon their conduct with respect to the performance of their duty, and behaviour to each other, in allowing proper salaries to their curates, &c. would not be of infinitely more benefit and advantage to the community, than their attendance in parliament, where they, at present, only serve as dead weights in the scale, to sanction every measure of administration, however impolitic. As matters are at present conducted, our bishops, by visiting their dioceses, and making so short a residence, are in a manner, not only total strangers to the laity, but even to the clergy, I mean the inferior part of them, upon whom the care of all the souls of their dioceses is devolved. I have always understood, that their lordships sat in the upper house of parliament, to watch over, and take care that nothing passed to the detriment of the established church, and to promote the affairs of the clergy; as well as to assist in enacting other laws for the benefit of the realm.

But has it ever yet been known, that their lordships made *one* motion, since they have enjoyed the privilege of sitting in that house, that tended to the advancement of religion and the benefit of the established church; by placing the present distressed, most useful body of people, the inferior clergy, upon such a footing, as might be a means of maintaining themselves with any degree of comfort and decency,

cency, and thereby attracting more respect and attention to their ministry, doctrine, and example?

It is the duty of bishops to inspect into the affairs of the clergy of their respective diocesses, the very word in the Greek implies it; but a continuance in the metropolis, in attending the levees of the great in pursuit of translations, is totally incompatible with this weighty concern, to see that the duty of every parish is duly performed, and properly attended to; and where the principal does not attend in person, that a proper salary be allowed, that they be not *oppressed and devoured* by each other, as is too frequently the case. A curate, with the most incompetent salary, is as worthy of the protection, respect, and care of his diocesan, as the loftiest dignified pluralist. St. Paul obliges Timothy, who was bishop of Ephesus, *to do every thing impartially, without preferring one before another*. St. Peter, in his exhortation to the elders of the churches, seems to have comprised all that can be desired upon this head; *Feed the flock of God,* says he, *which is among you, taking the oversight thereof, not by constraint,*

straint, *but unwillingly; not for filthy lucre, but of a ready mind; neither as being Lords over God's heritage*: that is, not using despotic authority, or partiality in your dioceses. It is evident that these passages imply, that every bishop should consider himself as a common father to his clergy in general, and bound to conduct all matters with an equitable, impartial hand among them; not bestowing all preferment upon such as have already *too much*, and much more than they think proper to attend to, by the recommendation of great men in power; or at the nod of the minister of the state: but, to pay some regard to abilities, proficiency in learning, long service in the vineyard, such as are burthened with large families, moral character, and in distressed circumstances. But daily experience convinces us, that the reverse of this is the present practice.

> Preferment now goes by letter and affection,
> And not by old gradation,
> Where each second stood heir to the first.
>
> SHAKESPEARE.

In the military profession it is esteemed extremely unjust, and a great degradation, to place a young stripling over the head of an old experienced veteran; and why not in the church militant?

Another particular I esteem extremely reprehensible in our bishops, is, their engaging TOO DEEPLY IN POLITICKS, and their too great subserviency in seconding the views of the court and administration.

A notorious and fatal instance of this we have experienced, in their servile conduct in parliament in the course of the American war: I remember, during that impolitic, unjust, cruel, expensive, bloody contest, the whole bench of bishops voted uniformly for every question that favoured the views of administration; excepting Dr. Shipley, the late bishop of St. Asaph, and Dr. Hinchcliffe, the present bishop of Peterborough, who refused to *bow the knee to Baal*; to sacrifice their consciences to interest, I mean translations to better bishopricks.

During

During that iniquitous war, a prelate implicitly attached to the court, in whose diocese I have a small benefice, upon being informed that I had wrote a variety of papers reprobating the conduct of the minister of that period, and his venal tools in that business, told me, that it was wrong in a person of my profession to write upon political subjects; that it became me to write upon subjects of morality and divinity only: But the event has shewn, that my writing against the continuance of that iniquitous war, and pointing out the injustice and destructive consequence of it, was *right*; and his lordship voting to promote it, proved eventually *wrong*. In matters of life and death, where the life of a single individual only is concerned, it is usual for the prelates to retire; but in that bloody, ruinous war, where the lives of many thousands were depending, I am sorry to say it, they were as forward as the temporal lords to second that infamous minister to promote blood and slaughter.

I cannot avoid relating an anecdote of the Earl of Granville, father of the last Earl, when in the laſt reign a ſtruggle lay between him and the Pelhams, for the important office of firſt Lord of the Treaſury. His Lordſhip having, upon ſome occaſion, dropt an expreſſion in the courſe of debate, reflecting in ſome reſpect upon the bench of biſhops—in coming from the houſe, one of them aſked him, How he could expect ſupport from their order, by treating them ſo diſreſpectfully, ſhould he come to have the chief adminiſtration of affairs? His Lordſhip's anſwer was ſarcaſtical, " that if he ſhould have occaſion for their ſupport, he knew by what means it was to be acquired."—Hinting at their views of tranſlations.

The ingenious worthy biſhop of Landaff ingenuouſly acknowledges, that the fear of offending cramps the diſpoſition for adviſing ſincerely and honeſtly, to ſtop the career in extravagance and folly in elevated ſituations. That the influence of the crown is dangerous, when it extends to the deliberations of the hereditary counſellors of the ſtate, or the parliamentary repreſentatives of the people, *which*

for

for some time past has been increasing, and which should be diminished. His Lordship adds farther, that had *the influence of the crown been less predominant;* had the measures of the cabinet been canvassed with wisdom, by men exercising their free powers of deliberation, honestly for the common weal, America, the brightest jewel of his Majesty's crown, would not have been rudely severed from its parent stock. It is the curse of kings to be attended by slaves, who take their humour for a warrant, and who, to be endeared to their master, make no conscience of destroying his honor!

The prelates who promoted the business of that administration, have no reason to be offended with me for animadverting upon their political conduct, since they are condemned by one of their own order, and indeed by the *disinterested* part of the whole kingdom.

Another more recent instance of court servility and adulation in the prelates, was, in the publication of that memorable form of prayer, in which they attributed the King's malady to the sins and iniquities of his people.

Had

Had this happened some centuries past, in those dark ages, when monkish ignorance, bigotry, and superstition reigned in this kingdom, and all knowledge and learning was confined to the clergy only; it would not have been so much to be wondered at: but in times so enlightened as the present; when philosophy, the sciences, every branch of literature, and liberality of sentiment so remarkably flourish, and are diffused through all ranks of persons, in an equal, and in many of the laity in a superior degree to the prelates themselves; it was an insult to every man of sense and understanding through the whole kingdom, and as such, was severely reprobated and universally condemned.

Another very culpable conduct in our prelates, is, their interfering in contested elections; which is contrary to the laws of the constitution, that a peer should interfere with the commons; and I remember one of them, Dr. Maddox, when bishop of St. Asaph, being obliged to make humiliating concessions before the House, for sending circular letters to the clergy of his diocese, to influence them to vote for the court candidate Mr. Middleton, in opposition to Sir Watkin Williams Wynn, a gentleman of the first independence in principles and fortune: The bishop's motive for taking so active a part in that business, was to induce the corrupt minister of that day, to translate him to the see of Worcester.

The late bishop of Hereford, a weak man, at the last general election, acted the same part in favour of the contractor Mr. Harley, the court candidate and tool of Lord North; who had the most ample share of the spoils of the American war of any man in the House of Commons. To his honour and credit be it spoken, the present bishop of the see of Hereford, to shew his disapprobation of the conduct of his predecessor, has declared publicly to his clergy, that he will, upon no consideration whatever, desire to influence them in the choice of a representative, being determined never to interfere in any contest of that kind.

kind. Let it be obferved, that I do not mean Dr. Harley, who was bifhop of that fee only for a very fhort period, but a former prelate.

I could point out another *more recent inftance;* but as it would appear invidious, I chufe to decline it.

The encouragement our bifhops give to pluralities, and the connivance at non-refidence of the opulent clergy, is attended with the worft confequence to the caufe of religion; for if the clergy were obliged to refide, and lived more fuitable to their function, there would be lefs infidelity in men of high rank, and lefs immorality in thofe of low rank. The clergy may be confidered as a little leaven preferving from corruption the whole mafs; *their light would fhine before men as examples.*

With refpect to the diftribution of ecclefiaftical preferment, it muft be allowed, that fome inequality is neceffary, as rewards for extraordinary merit and ability; in the apoftle's fenfe of mankind, *fome were worthy of double honour;* but it muft be obferved, that the

apoftle

apostle *regards honour, and not filthy lucre;* and this honour or distinction, the dignities in our church are, in the opinion of most men, amply sufficient to answer the end, and in fact were so intended in the eye of the law, without the inequalities of pluralities.

To answer then the *original* intention of promoting religion, and the happiness of mankind; let each person have *one* benefice, a competent maintenance for the cure of souls, *and no more;* and with respect to deanries, arch-deaconries, prebends, and other honourable offices in the church, let them be as encouragements to men of superior learning: this would be surely a fitter and more proper distribution, than now exists among the sons of the church; where we see some living in the greatest indigence, *and eating the bread of affliction;* whilst others, often of less merit, are glutted with *too much preferment, and performing the duty of none.* I cannot avoid quoting Bishop Burnet's sentiments in his pastoral care, to this purpose:
Since,

Since, fays he, all the returns of obedience and refpect, efteem and fupport, are declared in Scripture to be due to the clergy, on account of *their watching over, and feeding the flock of God:* thofe who pretend to thefe, without confidering themfelves under the other obligations, are guilty of the worſt of facrilege, in devouring the things that are *facred*, without performing the duties for which they are due; and what right foever the laws of the land give them to poffefs them, yet, agreeable to the divine law, thofe who *do not wait at the altar, ought not to be partakers with the altar; thofe who do not minifter about holy things, ought not to live of the things of the temple; nor ought thofe who do not preach the gofpel, live of the gofpel.*

AVARICE is another fault imputed to the bifhops of our church by the laity. Amaffing great wealth from the revenues of their fees, often to enrich fuch as have no occafion for it; never employing any part for the augmenting fome of the poor vicarages, which are

are an insufficient maintenance for the incumbents; and relieving some of the distressed curates who labour under difficulties and embarrassments for want of competent salaries, is a disgrace to a Bishop. It is related of the bishop of Durham, Dr. Chandler, that he was so sensible of this, that he declared in his last moments, that he died SHAMEFULLY RICH; this was his expression: intimating that he was culpable in not having applied the superflux of his immense income from the church in works of charity, in relieving his distressed brethren, &c.

Notwithstanding what is advanced respecting the scantiness of the church revenue for the maintenance of the clergy of the established church in this kingdom, were pluralities abolished, and a more impartial distribution of preferments by our bishops to take place; were *dispensations, options, simoniacal contracts, resignations ad favorem, commendams,* and many other abuses connived at by our spiritual governors, reformed; and the clergy put

put in some degree upon the same footing with the Gallic church since the revolution; that is, a competency to *each individual* to maintain himself with decency; but superfluity to promote luxury, and profligacy to *none*; and a less inequality and disproportion through the *whole* than prevailed before, when the government was despotic and arbitrary: I say, was such a reform adopted amongst us in this kingdom, it would tend greatly to promote religion, by placing the clergy in general in a more respectable situation in the esteem and and opinion of the laity, who wish to see a better regulation take place, and are at this time forming associations to bring a bill into parliament for this purpose.

Whatever our spiritual governors may suppose, respecting the liberty and discretion they may have of exercising partiality in the distribution of preferment, in compliance with the applications of great men in power; yet they are all servants of the state, and *entrusted with* that power, which should be dispensed with equity and justice, as may best promote the

the caufe of God and religion *only*, and not to gratify their private views and fecular interefts; and for which every rational perfon muft be perfuaded, that they will be accountable at the final day of retribution.

It is aftonifhing with what avidity, with what fervile compliances, fome of our prelates are obferved to folicit the minifter to promote them to fome more valuable preferment. One would be difpofed to imagine, that a perfon, from being originally a curate, or fellow of a college of forty or fifty pounds a year, when elevated by fome fortunate recommendation to the epifcopal dignity, with a revenue of four or five thoufand pounds a year, might efteem himfelf happy, and fufficiently fortunate and contented, without having his reftlefs eye continually caft towards the richer fees of Winchefter or Durham, or afpiring to one of the arch-bifhopricks.

I cannot avoid relating an anecdote, which fhews the pliancy and time-ferving difpofition of the prelates, as well as their ingratitude to their benefactor; which I well remember, and can vouch for as a fact.—The late duke of Newcastle, when at the head of affairs in administration, opposed the then heir apparent, the prince of Wales, his present Majesty's father, for the chancellorship of the university of Cambridge: the duke's interest in the senate, on account of his having the disposal of all ecclesiastical preferments, appeared superior to that of the prince's, that he declined the contest; upon which the duke was elected. In recompence for the zeal of his party he rewarded them with different preferments; prebends, deaneries, and bishopricks. In a word, nearly all the bench of bishops owed their CREATION to his Grace: but no sooner was he divested of the high office of First Lord of the Treasury, viz. Prime Minister, by the intrigues of the late Earl of Bute, the then reigning favourite, than all the bishops, who constantly before attended his levee, instantly deserted him; which induced a facetious wag to remark, that all the bishops had forgot their CREATOR.

A certain worthy, ingenious prelate, who condefcended to perufe my manufcript when preparing for the prefs, candidly acknowledged that the cafe was as I related it; but in excufe for his brethren, he faid, it was owing to a miftake in the appointment of the levee-day, after the duke's difmiffion from office, that it happened that none of them attended.

Notwithftanding our bifhops are fenfible that the burthen of the miniftry lies entirely upon the fubftitute curates, the principals being abfent, hunting about in queft of additional preferment, and making what they enjoy *livings and emoluments* in the moft carnal fenfe of the words. It is aftonifhing how it comes to be fo fmall a part of the epifcopal duty (fince the church has made it part of her injunctions) to examine, or at leaft make fome little enquiry, into the abilities of thefe fubftitutes, who fupply the place of the incumbents who have, in a manner, deferted their flocks, as beneath their care or notice; whether

ther they be properly qualified for the bufinefs affigned them, and in which they are engaged; whether they be of good moral characters; whether they be allowed a fufficient falary by their employer; and whether they be able, by their learning, to expel errors, to withftand gain-fayers, and to inftruct their congregations in their religious duties, fo *that they be be able to give to every man that afketh, an anfwer of the faith* and hope that is in them. But the truth is, that our bifhops in general are total ftrangers to this body of men, upon whom the whole burden of the duty lies; thefe fubalterns in the church, *thefe hewers of wood and drawers of water,* are below the notice or cognizance of their fpiritual governors. The management and treatment of the fubftitutes is left entirely to the incumbents; who introduce them from different diocefes, without the leaft knowledge of the ordinary, or *any teftimonial whatever* refpecting their conduct and ability, from the *laft* place where they performed duty; for *cheapnefs* is the principal recommendation with the incumbents;

bents; proficiency in learning, moral conduct, proper addrefs, being free from uncouth awkward dialect, suitable voice, graceful manner of performing the duty, &c. these are only *secondary considerations* not worth regarding; this is in general the cafe, which, for various fubftantial and weighty reafons I could affign, *should not be fo*. What is above ftated is fo notorious, that there have been inftances of perfons officiating in the eftablifhed church, and this for fome time before they have been detected, *even in the metropolis*, who never received ordination. The worthy bifhop of London is now made fo fenfible of this, that he is determined, I am informed, to put a fpeedy end to it within *his diocefe*, which is of more importance, and more requifite than in any *other* in the kingdom, for obvious reafons.

The above abufe is the effect of the nonrefidence of our bifhops, who by their fhort continuance in their refpective dioceses where their duty lies, and for the fuperintendance and regulation of their clergy of every degree,

are

are so very amply rewarded by the state, whose servants they are: so that if they properly reflect, they are answerable for their neglect, both to God and the state in reality, and are guilty of a *kind of sacrilege* in receiving the revenues of the church, without performing the duties required of them.

It must be admitted, that nothing of this can be applicable to the bishop of London, as he is constantly resident where his duty requires. After the accession of worldly honor, and the erection of bishopricks into baronies (which was, upon the first institution, intended for a *political purpose* rather than any extraordinary favor to the church) episcopal residence became diminished, and a necessary attendance on the king's council or parliament; by which distant provincial dioceses, as is at present the case, became deserted and neglected. Whether the church, and religion in general, receives more benefit or detriment on that account, is no difficult matter to determine.

The ingenious liberal-minded bishop of Landaff, in a letter he addressed to the late archbishop of Canterbury, and to the legislature in general, among other reasons he assigns for an ecclesiastical reform, by rendering the bishopricks less disproportionate than they are at present: one is, a longer residence of the bishops in their respective dioceses; from which, he says, the best consequences might be expected.

For when the temptation to wish for translations were in a great measure removed, it would be natural for the bishops in general to consider themselves as settled for life in the sees to which they should be first appointed; this consideration would induce them to render their places of residence more comfortable and commodious; and an opportunity of living more comfortable, would beget an inclination to reside more constantly in them. Being wedded, as it were, to a particular diocese, they would think it expedient, of course, to become better acquainted with their clergy; and

by

by being better acquainted with their clergy, their situations, prospects, tempers, and talents, they would be better able to co-operate with them in the great work of amending the morals of his Majesty's subjects, and of *feeding the flock of Christ*. It is the duty of Christian Pastors in general, and of the principal pastors, the Bishops, in particularly, *to strengthen that member of the flock which is diseased, to heal that which is sick, to bind up that which is broken, to bring again that which is driven away, and to seek that which is lost*. That these and other parts of the pastoral office can never be so well performed as when the shepherd is *resident* in the midst of his flock, can admit no question. It is astonishing to conceive what beneficial influence the examples of the bishops, residing in their dioceses, and letting *their light shine before men*, who would be disposed to observe it, would have upon the lives of both clergy and laity.

I recollect a *certain bishop*, remarkable for his short residence in his diocese, just sufficient to enable

enable him to settle for the revenue of his see, holding two benefices in COMMENDAM, the most valuable in that diocese. This I esteem a species of sacrilege, engrossing a superfluity of what others stand so much in need of, and *performing the duties of neither*; it is to be observed, that the revenue of that see is now valued at between four and five thousand pounds a year. A sly farmer who rented the tythes, in conversation with the same bishop's curate, who officiated in one of the two livings he held in commendam, asked him, when he expected the CHIEF SHEPHERD down amongst them? Upon the curate's answering, That he was ignorant of his Lordship's intention of visiting his diocese: I suppose, replied the farmer, with a sarcastic look and sneer, *about the time of shearing, about the time of shearing!* intimating, as if the chief shepherd had no farther care or concern about the flock than to receive the FLEECES, that is, the emoluments. The very same bishop who held these two livings in commendam, at the same time giving *strict orders* in his charge to his clergy, at a visitation,

sitation, that no person should officiate in his diocese, in more than one church upon any pretence whatever. This was cruelty in the extreme, and the height of oppression, to prevent a person from endeavouring to support himself and family by his diligence and application to the duties of his function, to increase his *small pittance* of income from his salary; when his diocesan enjoyed several hundred pounds a year from his commendams, *without cure of souls,* exclusive of his ample revenue from his fee. *Non missura cutem, nisi plena cruoris hirudo.*

Were COMMENDAMS abolished the poorer bishops would be freed from the necessity of holding ecclesiastical preferments with their bishopricks; consequently there would be more provision for the rest of the clergy, and not so much obloquy and reflection upon the bishops for their avarice, ambition, &c. Rendering the bishopricks in general something more upon an equality, or not quite so disproportionate as at present obtains, would put an end totally to this evil in the church. What can be more unreasonable and absurd, than that a bishop of Ely should have a revenue from his see of between seven and eight thousand pounds a year; a bishop of Winchester between nine and ten thousand; and the bishop of Durham about twelve thousand a year upon an average: what a disproportion between the bishoprick of Bristol, *only* about four hundred pounds a year; the bishoprick of Landaff about seven or eight hundred; and St. David's, I believe, of less value: I cannot be very accurate in this statement, it being quite impossible; but the value of the three latter, contrasted against the three former, is sufficient to point out the necessity of a reform in ecclesiastical affairs, amongst us of this kingdom, which the legislative body have a right, and are fully competent at any time to accomplish; and indeed it is what would be brought about, was there an equal representation of the people in parliament; but while things are in the present state, it is not to be expected; being morally impossible, while every kind of reform

reform is refifted by the minifter and his dependents.

Another confequence, and that not the leaft, of the bifhopricks being lefs difproportionate in point of value of revenue, would be a greater independence of the bifhops in the houfe of lords, they would be lefs under the influence of the minifter, was there no profpect or expectation of tranflations to better bifhopricks, the *temptation would be removed;* their obedience to the nod of the minifter during the American war, will fuffice to exemplify this moft glaringly, as well as fatally; their conduct in that bufinefs (whatever they may think of the matter) has greatly lowered them in the efteem and veneration of both laity and clergy through the whole community, which is not very eafily regained and recovered; the people are more keen-fighted, and fhrewd in their remarks and obfervations, than their fuperiors in rank and ftation imagine.

Would our bifhops unanimoufly agree in a refolution to admit none into the church who

were

were remarkable for their perſonal deformity; nor any but graduates who had undergone a regular education in either of the two univerſities, it would be attended with the beſt conſequence to the cauſe of religion amongſt us. The profeſſion would become more reſpectable in the opinion of the laity, were there not ſo many ſupernumerary expectants of mean appearance, and uncouth provincial dialects, &c. which often excite rather ridicule than ſeriouſneſs and devotion in our congregations where they officiate. It is in a great meaſure owing to the biſhops of Landaff and St. David's, that the ſouthern part of the kingdom is ſo over-run with perſons of the above deſcription. There are in South Wales charity or free ſchools, where poor people ſend their ſons to be inſtructed in a little Latin and Greek, juſt ſufficient to undergo an examination for orders; and as they are not in a capacity of defraying the expence of a liberal univerſity education, application is made to one of the above biſhops to ordain them. Theſe biſhops, with the beſt intention, being ſenſible

ble that there are several churches and chapels in their dioceses, that will not support gentlemen who have had the advantages of a regular university education, that their congregations may not be entirely neglected, ordain the above description of persons to officiate in them. No sooner are these poor humble suppliants admitted into the church, than their ambition prompts them to quit the barren mountains of Wales in exchange for the metropolis and its environs, where they instantly put themselves upon a level with the regular graduates of our universities, who have spent hundreds of pounds upon their education. Carmarthen is the place that furnishes the greatest part of these persons.

There are two additional reasons, *at present*, why so many persons should not be admitted into orders in the established church. The one is, the loss of America, which before was furnished with a considerable number of our supernumerary clergy, who had no prospect of preferment in the mother country: the other is, the prospect of a long continuance of of peace, being under no apprehension of either a continental or naval war, which at other times engaged no inconsiderable number of the inferior part of our clergy as assistant chaplains to regiments, and chaplains to men of war.

As our commerce to India is now become so very considerable, and vessels of much larger size and bulk now employed than ever before, should the legislature in their wisdom think proper to put the trade, and the very extensive territories we possess in Indostan, into the hands of government, at the expiration of the charter of the East India Company. I humbly presume to *hint only*, whether there would be any impropriety in enacting a statute, that every vessel employed in that trade should receive a chaplain, as well as ships of war: I cannot conceive what objection could be made to the adopting such a regulation, which I am of opinion, could not fail of being attended with very good consequence.

Let it be seriously adverted to, that in pointing out the above abuses occasioned by the

the conduct of our prelates; it is by no means the intention of the author of thefe fheets to degrade or difparage that venerable order, by fpeaking ill of dignities; far otherwife: but with a view of benefiting religion, and placing the reft of the clergy in a more refpectable light in the opinion of the laity, in order to add more weight and attention to their miniftration. The author humbly prefumes, there will be, in the courfe of this fmall treatife, a variety of other abufes and hints, which, would their Lordfhips condefcend to pay attention to, might tend greatly to the advantage of the eftablifhed church; fuch as they, from their elevated ftations can have no cognizance of, and which may be eafily remedied. Whatever has been hinted at, refpecting the rendering the bifhopricks lefs difproportionate in value and patronage, &c. it is not intended it fhould affect any perfon now living; but agreeable to the learned and ingenious bifhop of Landaff's fcheme, of appropriating, *as they become vacant only*, one third, or fome definitive part of the income of every deanery, prebend,

prebend, or canonry of the churches of Westminster, Windsor, Christ-church, Canterbury, Worcester, Durham, Norwich, Ely, Peterborough, Carlisle, &c. to the same purpose, *mutatis mutandis*, as the first fruits and tenths were appropriated by the act passed the fifth of Queen Anne. Whoever wishes to be farther acquainted with his Lordship's proposal, I refer them to the Letter itself, which had so little attention paid to it, notwithstanding its reasonableness and good tendency.

There is nothing in what is proposed by the author in these sheets that may be esteemed speculative or chimerical, but plain stubborn facts, which cannot be controverted, which the laity of every denomination are sensible of, and regret; such as may be redressed without apprehension of danger; and would be of infinite advantage to the community in general. Here is nothing to excite fear or discontent to our prelates who enjoy the rich bishopricks. Nothing to occasion panick, or the least dread or apprehension to the Pitts, the Grenvilles, the Dundasses, the Burkes

Burkes *also now*, &c. &c. &c. the numerous adherents to the minister, who may enjoy great emoluments in peace and security, without having recourse to ring the changes upon the words chimerical, reform, innovation, impolitic and improper *at this time*, visionary speculation, *dangerous now*, &c. &c. &c. in terrorem; in a word, from any thing touched in this little work they have nothing to fear, let them eat their loaves and fishes in security, they will not be disturbed. The avowed object of this publication is to promote religion, morality, and good order, and not sedition, &c.

PART THE SECOND.

Treats of the Conduct of the INCUMBENTS,—*the* PLURALISTS.

S<small>T</small>. CHRISOSTOM, in his treatise *de Sacerdotio*, among a variety of other particulars, observes, that the honour and respect that accrue to the clergy from their administrations, are common to all who have received ordination. Difference in point of preferment makes none in their power and authority in performing the duties of the church; the incumbent and his curate are upon an equality in the exercise of their functions; whether it be in the desk, font, pulpit, or at the altar. The clergy then, in general, beneficed or otherwise, are upon a level *as ministers of Christ, and stewards of the mysteries of God.*

There is a mistake among the vulgar part of the laity, of a very mortifying nature, respecting

specting the persons who act in the capacity of curates; and that is, their being considered and treated as *servants* to the opulent pluralist, whereas the inferiority consists only in point of the provision of the church revenue, and not in their administrations, as before observed.

Every clergyman, from his education and profession, is, by the constitution of this kingdom, placed upon the footing and rank of a gentleman, for the furtherance of his function. Such a one acting in the subordinate station of assistant to a beneficed clergyman of the same order, is totally different from all other deputies or substitutes whatever, in secular employs.

The most honourable and exalted station in our church, the archbishop of Canterbury, the metropolitan of England, is open to a curate of the lowest degree in point of salary, should he have recommendation sufficiently powerful with the Sovereign, the fountain of all honours and dignities.

There are many imperious, illiberal pluralists, who, to aggrandize themselves, and indulge their pride and vanity, are content to observe their assistants degraded in the eyes of the laity; but I would recommend to this oppressed body of men, not to betray the privileges of their function by any servile compliances, or unbecoming submission. Too much condescension in a clergyman is generally misinterpreted, and supposed to proceed not from humility and good breeding, but from a consciousness of his inferiority; and others are willing to allow him so much sense, as to be a competent judge of his own inconsiderableness; therefore he is generally treated accordingly; according to the Italian adage,

Chi peccora si fa, il lupo se la mangia.

This contempt readily descends from the persons to the professions; so that the holy office becomes degraded, and the word of God blasphemed by such servility. St. Paul shews the greatness of his spirit, where he says, God has not given us the spirit of fear, but of power; that is, of christian courage and magnanimity.

There are no persons whatever whom a haughty supercilious carriage so ill becomes as clergymen. Their behaviour gives the lye direct to the doctrine they pretend to instil into others, as received, from Christ their master. There is a respect from the highest dignitary to the most distressed substitute; for it is a mercy and favor of Providence, that he, who now lolls at his ease and luxury, was not a miserable curate himself, starving upon the offals, in a manner, of his rich patron's table. A haughty demeanour defeats itself; and so far from acquiring respect, that it excites contempt and detestation. To insult, domineer, and treat an inferior imperiously, conciliates no esteem or affection; it may oblige a dependant to keep his distance; but it will be a distance without reverence; it may attract parasites and flatterers, but few faithful friends and admirers.

It

It is observed, no persons make harder bargains than the beneficed clergy, and particularly with their substitutes—their curates. It is no uncommon thing for a dignitary pluralist, who enjoys several hundreds a year from different preferments, to beat down an indigent curate, perhaps with a family, to officiate at the lowest stipend possible, not enabling him the means of supporting himself and family with any degree of decency; and at the same time stipulating with him strictly, with respect to presents received from the munificence and liberality of any of the opulent parishioners above the stated fees; even a hat-band and pair of gloves, upon attending a funeral, must not be reserved, at the peril of being dismissed from the cure; this in general is the case: there may be particular exceptions.

It is a practice in various parts of the kingdom, for two beneficed pluralists, whose parishes are not at an inconvenient distance, to join together to procure a person to serve both churches, at twenty or twenty-five pounds a year

year each; when each of the benefices *singly*, might well enable the incumbent to pay an assistant liberally; this is what is stiled, consolidating the curacies, if I may be allowed a ludicrous expression, and why not? The facetious *Horace* says, RIDENTEM DICERE VERUM, QUID VETAT?

Another manœuvre frequently practised in clerical affairs by the pluralists, is, curtailing the parishioners of the afternoon's service (whose souls they had solemnly promised to watch over, &c.) in order to have the church served at a *cheaper* rate. This is the cause of so many persons of the established church deserting it, and resorting to methodist meetings, &c. &c.

The ordinary *is a total stranger to these petty concerns, being so busily engaged in other matters*, that he is in a manner a stranger to his diocese. I appeal to the clergy in general for the truth of what is advanced, and that this statement of things is not exaggerated, but literally true, of which there are a great variety of instances.

It is generally remarked, that the dignified pluralists scarce ever deign to perform divine service, when they annually visit their parishioners to settle for their tythes, &c. this is esteemed a kind of degradation; they may condescend to give them a sermon, as the phrase is, but reading divine service is esteemed by them a kind of drudgery fit only for the curate. In plain English, they consider themselves too great to perform the office of their substitute: that is, to address the Deity in prayer in behalf of those whose souls they had in the most solemn manner promised at their institution to watch over, and prepare for a future state; but they will display their vanity, by delivering, perhaps a composition of another person of superior abilities, as their own; in recompence for some hundred pounds a year received from their parishioners, before their return to the metropolis, Bath, or some fashionable place of gay resort.

This brings to my recollection an anecdote of a dignitary pluralist, a Doctor Morgan, who was presented to a rectory in Leicestershire.

shire. He arrived in this Parish the latter part of the week, was inducted, and on Sunday gave his parishioners a sermon, and on Monday returned to town. His curate, a Mr. Watts, a gentleman of some humour, knowing that the Doctor never intended to reside amongst them, or probably ever visit them more; told the parishioners to their great surprize, that the Doctor had preached his *farewell sermon*; and in fact it proved so, for he never saw their faces more; but took care to have the rent of the glebe, tythes, &c. remitted to him with great punctuality. Thus this *conscientious* gentleman *undertook the cure of souls*.

It is astonishing that the opulent pluralists do not act more liberally to their brethren, who all must have once been in the abject state of curates themselves, upon their first entering into orders; the nature of a title for orders implies it, fellows of colleges only exempted; and besides a clergyman, it is amazing they should be so forgetful of the first rule in morality, *of doing to others as they*

H *would*

would wish to be done to, were they in the situation of curates. It is to be observed that the legislature, not foreseeing the extraordinary difference in the value of money, alteration in the mode of living, the price of provisions; as well as the great improvement in the value of the rectories where inclosures have taken place, some doubled, some trebled in value, left the wealthy incumbents to their own generosity; little supposing they would be wanting in acting liberally towards their brethren of the same education, the same expectations, and the same profession.

It never was intended, that the church revenue should be so disposed as to aggrandize *some*, and starve others; much less that the incumbent who performed *none* of the duty, and took not the least care of the souls entrusted to him, should enjoy nearly the *whole income*, whilst the *real labourer in the vineyard* received not a pittance sufficient to sustain him: this is literally *muzzling the ox that treadeth out the corn*, with a vengeance!

This

This disproportion among the clergy of the established church, is the universal subject of conversation; every serious well disposed person deplores the incompetent provision assigned to the greatest part of them; but no person attempts to seek redress in a parliamentary way for so great a grievance; although one of the most important national concern, when properly reflected upon.\ With respect to our bishops, and dignitaries in general, they dread the very idea of a better regulation in the church, lest their great incomes should be diminished, as much as administration and the dependents of the minister do a reform in parliament, by a more equal representation of the people.

There is a common practice that prevails with the gay part of incumbents, to avoid residence among their parishioners, whose souls they promised, in the most solemn manner, to take care of at their institution, to obtain leave of absence from the bishop in whose diocese their benefices are situated; and should there be any difficulty of obtaining (which very rarely

rarely happens) application is made to some Peer's valet-de-chambre for the purchase of a scarf, that is, an appointment to be his Lordship's chaplain; and should that Peer be full, having the complement that the law allows, one of them is desired to resign *pro tempore*, to serve the present purpose. This being accomplished, the incumbent is then at liberty to reside where his inclination leads him, while the flock is deserted, and left to the care of the hireling. This is a very great abuse amongst the incumbents; for this privilege was originally intended to Peers, for their domestic chaplains *only*, who are to reside *bona fide* in the family. There are many non-resident incumbents, who thus leave the care of the souls of their neglected parishioners to their curates, who sing *requiem* to their consciences, upon the presumption that they have disburthened themselves of the whole charge, and that the substitute is answerable for all defaults; and that if *one soul perish for lack of knowledge*, God will require *the blood of that soul at his hand*. A very scanty reward indeed

indeed for fo much danger, was that the cafe; but the eternal rule is this, *he that receiveth much, of him shall much be required*; a maxim founded in equity it is, that the benefice shall go with the office and duty.

The rules of religion require perfonal fervice, and oblige thofe *who live by the altar to wait at the altar*, where the original word προσεδρευειν fignifies *refiding*, and it is ufed by a perfon of no lefs eminence than St. Chryfoftom, to the prefent purpofe.

The laws of the church are moft of them comprized in the fenfe of the council of Mentz, that *one man's holding more benefices than one, is extremely mifchievous in the church*; as one perfon cannot perform the offices they require. Even the law of the land, that famous ftatute of the 21ft of Henry the VIIIth, in which the pluralifts place their chief confidence, was originally intended to prevent the great evil of pluralities, and to *oblige refidence*; however, the many provifions for perfons qualified for difpenfations may have deftroyed the force of it; but be that as it may,

✗ at our ordinations we promise most solemnly, in all respects, to take care of the people that shall at any time be committed to our charge; and at our institution to any benefice, there is a *certain particular* people appointed us, and we undertake *the cure of their souls*, without restriction, or the least reserve. If then our faith, given in express words to God and his church, can bind; if promises made at the altar do oblige; if a stipulation, in consideration of which orders are given, and institutions granted us, is sacred, our obligation, in point of conscience, continues the same, as if no dispensation had been granted.

✗ There is another abuse among avaricious incumbents which is sometimes practised; and that is, selling titles for orders to young candidates, either for a sum of money, or upon condition of their serving the church for which the title is given, without salary, for a stipulated time: added to this, the same incumbent signs the testimonial requisite for the candidate, and perhaps procures two more of his friends to do the same, answering for his proficiency

ficiency in learning, moral character, and conduct, for three years paft, as required by the bifhop of the diocefe; when probably the candidate in queftion has not been known to either of them above a few days; and fo far from having had a regular univerfity education, that he is no other than a writing ufher in fome petty fchool, or fome *gifted infpired methodift*, who declines working at a mechanical bufinefs, &c. Having mentioned the abufe of granting falfe titles to improper perfons for orders, it may not be unfeafonable here to explain this, as it was cuftomary in the firft ages of the church. For many *ages* then, none was ordained to the priefthood, who had not at the fame time a particular cure affigned him: antiquity knew no diftinction between ordination and a benefice. From the firft eftablifhment of the church till the year 500, no perfon was ordained without a defignation to fome particular benefice for his fure *maintenance*. In procefs of time, a little latitude began to take place in this refpect, and the bifhops began to relax from this ftrict rule, by

ordaining

ordaining without title, in expectation of a benefice becoming vacant. In time these supernumerary co-adjutors to beneficed incumbents became so numerous, that a law was enacted, that the bishops were obliged to maintain all the clergy themselves whom they had ordained without title. *Episcopus si aliquem sine certo titulo de quo necessaria vitæ percipiat, in diaconum & presbyterum ordinaverit, tamdiu ei necessaria subministret, donec in aliqua ecclesia de convenientia stipendia militiæ clericalis assignet; nisi talis ordinatus de sua paterna hæreditate, vel aliqua alia honestatis causa subsidium possit habere.*

This canon was made by the council of Lateran, under Alexander the Third, and is to be found in the 4th chap. *de prebendis.*

I have never known an instance of any person claiming a maintenance, according to the express words of the title, and agreeable to the tenor of the canon above quoted; the words and sum specified in the title were esteemed by the generality of the incumbents as words of course, mere forms only; as they

they were seldom or never enforced, that I can recollect, till very lately; upon that memorable dispute which took place between Dr. Hynde, rector of St. Anne's, Soho, and his curate Mr. Martin, to whom he had given a title for ordination.

The Doctor was desirous of dismissing Mr. Martin from the cure, which he resisted, alledging, that he had a right to continue to officiate in that church as curate, according to the tenor of the words expressed in the title, *till he was provided with some ecclesiastical preferment.*

The Doctor was of a contrary opinion; so that the cause came to be argued in the Ecclesiastical Court, in Doctors Commons, and was determined in favour of Mr. Martin, the curate. This mortified Dr. Hynde to such a degree, that he contrived means of being removed to another benefice, that he might not perform duty in the same church with his curate, with whom he was at variance, and who had foiled him in this dispute. Mr. Martin maintained still farther, that he had a right,

right, by the words of the title, to be continued to officiate as curate in that church to any succeeding rector or incumbent there, as his designation was for that *particular church*.—This matter came to be tried in the court of Exchequer, but how it was determined I am at a loss to say.

There is another very great abuse and evil, which too frequently prevails in our church, which is SIMONY. Church Benefices are now purchased as openly as temporal property; which gives an opening to any person who has command of money, however ill qualified or immoral, of enjoying a considerable share of the revenue of the church, even without performance of duty. This is attended with another evil, of a serious and heinous nature, which is PERJURY.

As many of the laity may not be well acquainted with the nature of the simoniacal oath, I think it necessary to inform them, that it is the strictest of all the oaths administered in this realm. The clergyman upon his institution swears, that he *gave not the least consideration*

consideration whatever, either himself, directly nor indirectly, nor any person for him with his privity, knowledge, or consent; when perhaps he had been *personally* treating with the patron for the purchase, and even *present* at the payment of the money. I was witness to a notorious instance of a transaction of this kind in the diocese of Lincoln; where the patron and the person who was to be the incumbent of the benefice, were both together when the purchase money was paid; the latter took the simoniacal oath, which was tendered to him a few days after, without the least scruple, and resides now upon that benefice near Atherstone in Warwickshire.

There is another species of simony, which is stiled Petticoat Simony; when a clergyman, by marrying the niece or daughter of a bishop, becomes a pluralist of large income, his lady being portioned out of the revenue of the church. I could point out several persons now living, but it might appear invidious, therefore shall decline it; but one instance within my recollection was so notorious, that I cannot avoid mentioning it.

It was a dean of Canterbury, who by marrying Archbishop Potter's daughter, became possessed of Six or Seven different pieces of preferment, to the amount of above four thousand pounds a year of the church revenue, by way of marriage portion.

This was the gentleman who gave occasion to so many jokes and witticisms, and whom the celebrated Hogarth satirized in the print of the ass laden with preferment. But dull and heavy as the Dean was supposed to be, he had the address to blunt the keenness of raillery when attacked. Agreeable to the Italian adage, *l'asino pur pigro, stimolato, tira qualche calcio.*

Upon the publication of that print some officers of the guards, at St. James's Coffee-house, where the Dean usually frequented when in town, were desirous of having, as they expressed it, a little fun by smoaking the Dean, placed the print alluded to in a conspicuous part of the coffee-room, where it must

must unavoidably be observed. The Dean, upon viewing it with a crowd of those gentlemen about him, in expectation of seeing him much mortified and embarrassed, were mortified themselves upon the pleasant turn he gave the joke, by exclaiming aloud; "You see, gentlemen, Master Hogarth has represented me here, as *bending* under the weight of my different preferments; but he is much mistaken, I can bear a great deal more still." The officers shrunk off abashed, having missed their aim, and disappointed of their joke.

But the purchasing of benefices for money, and marrying the daughters or nieces of bishops, are not the only species of simoniacal contracts; that of selling titles for orders just touched upon, is as great an abuse as the two above-mentioned; and I am of opinion comes nearer the case of *Simon Magus*, which we read of in the New Testament, who gave rise to this expression.

COLLUSIVE RESIGNATIONS also are generally attended with simony and perjury: when we we hear of a person being presented to a benefice, upon the cession of another, we may conclude, in general, that *some consideration* has been given, that something of simony has been transacted.

This practice has these evils attending it: first it leads to the sin of perjury; and besides, is often the means of introducing an immoral and improper person by means of his money to the cure of souls, perhaps to the exclusion of a man of learning and merit, who might be an ornament to his profession, and who would probably have discharged the duty much more to the satisfaction and benefit of the parishioners.

Here I may add also, that patrons who dispose of benefices to improper persons do not sufficiently reflect, that this is a trust of a solemn nature lodged in their hands, *when they present a person to the cure of souls*; that it is a weighty concern for which they will be accountable to God; and that they will in a great measure be accountable for the souls that may be be loft, and whatever abufe may arife, through their corrupt contract, and improper choice.

Doctor Warner, in the Appendix to his Ecclefiaftical Hiftory, publifhed in 1757, has the following obfervation; " Of the nine " thoufand and fome hundred churches and " chapels, which we have in England and " Wales, fix thoufand are not above the value " of forty pounds a year." Doctor Burn has alfo ftated the number of fmall livings (in his Ecclefiaftical Law, article firft fruits and tenths) in the following terms—" The num-" ber of livings capable of augmentation " have been certified as follows; 1071 li-" vings not exceeding 10*l.* a year, 1467 li-" vings above 10*l.* and not exceeding 20*l.* a " year, 1126 livings above 20*l.* and not ex-" ceeding 30*l.* a year, 1049 livings above 30*l.* " and not exceeding 40*l.* a year, 884 livings " above 40*l.* and not exceeding 50*l.* a year. " So that in the whole there are 5597 livings " certified under 50*l.* a year."—This ftatement of the church revenue, I doubt not, will greatly

greatly astonish many of the laity, who never have turned their thoughts to this subject.

It is now very near 80 years when the return of livings was first made to the governors of Queen Anne's bounty. The bounty, assisted by private benefactions, has made a slow progress indeed since its commencement; so that the clergy in general who have received a share of it have been very little bettered in their condition, and particularly since the governors have thought proper to lower the rate of interest of the money due to the several claimants, from five per cent. to two per cent. which, I am sensible, was with a view of enabling them to augment yearly a greater number of benefices; but did they know the inconvenience many suffer upon this account, they would be probably surprized; while they themselves who have the management, enjoy large incomes from the church revenue, without ever feeling for the difficulties and distresses of their brethren who have been less fortunate in the church.

The

The reason that so many persons are obliged to *submit* to the above regulations of the governors, who are bishops of great incomes, is owing to the extreme difficulty of finding certain portions of land which must exactly suit the specific sum they are entitled to, together with the small sums received in aid of the bounty by private benefactions, &c. so that in fact the present generation of the inferior clergy must submit to be still distressed the more, in order to benefit those who are to succeed them several generations to come; and that this is the case I shall quote the following authorities:

Doctor Warner says, it will be 500 years before every living in this kingdom can be advanced, *by the present management of Queen Anne's bounty*, to the value of 60*l.* a year. And Doctor Burn has calculated, that supposing the clear amount of the bounty to make 55 augmentations yearly, it will be 339 years, from the year 1714 (which was the first year in which any augmentations were made) before all the livings in the established church amongſt us, can exceed 53*l.* a year. And if it be computed that half of ſuch augmentations may be made in conjunction with other benefactions, which is improbable, it will require 226 years before all the livings already certified will exceed 50*l.* a year.

As the private benefactions are found to be ſo very few among the laity, ſuppoſe the biſhops who enjoy ſeveral thouſands a year of the church revenue, for the performance of ſcarce any duty to the benefit of the community, would there be any impropriety ſhould they apply *ſome part* yearly towards augmenting the vicarages of the leaſt value in their reſpective dioceſes, in conjunction with Queen Anne's bounty, in order to accelerate the end propoſed by that charity, by way of ſetting an example to the laity; ſhould they adopt ſo laudable a reſolution, it would only be returning to the church from which it was acquired, the ſuperflux of what it ſo much wants, and what they themſelves can ſo well ſpare, and have ſo little occaſion for; and particularly ſuch of them as have no families, and

and have acquired *all they possess* from the church, of whom I can point out several instances, who never were possessed of any private patrimony whatever. What objection can so venerable a body make to so charitable and pious a purpose, the benefit of which would descend to infinite numbers for many generations to come, as well as comfort and relieve at present a great number of their cotemporary distressed brethren, who pine and languish for want of the conveniences of life, whilst their superiors live in luxury, ease, and the greatest pomp. And if this was copied also by our rich dignitary pluralists, it would operate more powerful still, and be a means of accelerating the augmentation of the poorer vicarages in a double or triplicate ratio, and induce the rich part of the laity, who have a regard for the church, to follow their example.

As it has been stated above, that the number of livings through the whole kingdom amounts to near ten thousand, and that near six thousand of these are under 50*l.* a year;

it may be concluded then, that the remaining part, amounting to about four thousand, are rectories, livings of value, such as are possessed by incumbents, generally pluralists; for let it be remembered, that the most *valuable benefices* are always such as are held by the pluralists, and often dignitaries, at the same time.

There have been near a thousand inclosures of Lordships, which were common fields, in the course of about 35 years past, which, in general, have doubled, some trebled the incomes of the incumbents. Notwithstanding the small vicarages are not bettered for the inferior part of the clergy; yet the rectories where there are great tythes, have been benefited in a very extraordinary degree.

It may be necessary to observe, that the valuation of benefices in the king's books, or the last valuation and improved value, give very little insight into the *present* real improved value of livings in general.

I remember the rectory of Doddington, in the isle of Ely, (the incumbent of which is Doctor Proby, dean of Litchfield) about eleven

ven hundred pounds a year, about 35 years ago, when I was a student in the university of Cambridge, having been upon the spot; but was informed by an inhabitant of the parish very lately, that it amounts at this time to above two thousand two hundred pounds a year, or more. The means by which Doctor Proby became possessed of that valuable benefice, does infinite credit and honour to the memory of the late Doctor Gooch, who was then bishop of that see. The dean of Litchfield, should he happen to peruse this, will understand readily what I allude to, it being too tedious to relate here.

I also remember, about the same time, the rectory of Hawarden, in the diocese of St. Asaph, and county of Flint, when a relation of mine was presented to it, no more than 400*l.* a year in value, but at this time amounts to above 1600*l.* the last incumbent was Sir Stephen Glynn, Baronet, the patron.

I am informed a proportionable advance has been made in the valuable living of Winwick, in the patronage of the earl of Derby.

⨯ In a word, every rectory through the kingdom has been confiderably advanced within the laft 35 years, even where there have not been inclofures; as the produce of every article the land produces have borne an extravagant price for fome time paft, and our improvement in agriculture, fuperior to that of any country in Europe, has made the moft rapid progrefs: foreigners from all parts have come here to copy our improved mode of cultivating every fpecies of foil, particularly from Ruffia by the emprefs's command, and at her expence.

What I would infer from the above ftatement, is, that the incumbents of livings fhould allow their fubftitutes, while they enjoy fuch plentiful incomes at their eafe, a falary in *fome degree proportionable* to the improvement of their benefices; and remember that *the labourer is worthy of his reward*, that a liberal income fhould infpire liberal fentiments: one might reafonably fuppofe, that one fourth of the value of a benefice would not be too much for thofe who oblige themfelves to continual refidence, *who fuftain the whole burden and*

and heat of the day, who in *labours are more abundant*, who, as matters are at present conducted, added to their spiritual concerns and fatigue, have the conflict of poverty to struggle with besides, and are obliged in all things to *approve themselves* the ministers of God, in *patience*, in *afflictions*, in *necessities*, in *distresses*; whilst the wealthy incumbents their employers, have often no farther view than to the emoluments, which they dissipate in luxury, &c. become estranged from their flocks, nor are solicitous what becomes of them, provided they can but *feed* themselves with the *fat*, and *cloath* themselves with the *wool*.

Besides a liberal salary allowed, a kind benevolent, and friendly behaviour from an incumbent towards his substitute, would be extremely becoming, where such connection in the performance of the duty of the church subsists between them, free from superciliousness and hauteur, speaking favourable of his attention to his duty, moral conduct, his ability, &c. This might be expected from men in such

happy

happy circumstances, and under such ties of mutual relations in the church. But when the reverse of this often appears; when we observe proud priests of large incomes, by pluralities, treat their dependent curates with an air of superiority, that would better become a Persian monarch than a christian clergyman. What shall we say for such men in excuse for their conduct? Shall we join in the calumnies of the enemies of our church, who impute this to the worst of causes, arrogance and pride, and a spirit of infidelity in our clergy.

Or shall we suppose that there is an external and internal doctrine in the Christian system; the one to be delivered and made public to the people, the other to be concealed and reserved by the clergy, for their own private practice, as is the case in the church of Rome.

This reprehensible conduct in some of our beneficed pluralists, is accounted for from the mode of life they have been accustomed to; such as fellows of colleges who have for several

several years led a recluse life, little conversant with the world; this, it is true, improves and adorns the faculties of the mind, by giving a man an opportunity of much reading and deep contemplation; but at the same time deprives him of the knowledge of the world, and insight into men and manners; and by that means renders him a pedant and sour misanthrope; the most odious despicable character in society; instead of a man of letters, civility, and polished manners. This disagreeable temper and demeanour is often the result of a hasty accumulation of preferments.

Preferments by collation, and estates by inheritance and acquisition, have this difference in their effects upon men in general; the former coming all at once, and sometimes unexpectedly, swell the heart, and intoxicate the head by too sudden success; the latter coming leisurely, and after some expectance, are usually received with temper and moderation, occasion no great alteration in the mind. ✢ What preferment such a person acquires, he imputes to his

his *own merit*; what he sees others less fortunate want, he attributes to *their* defects; those who are before him in the race and career for wealth and honour, he *emulates*; but such as are unsuccessful and behind him, *he despises*. Never reflecting *that the race is not always to the swift, nor the battle to the strong; neither yet bread to the wise, nor riches to men of understanding; nor yet favor to men of skill; but time and skill happen to all.*

— Enforcing the residence of incumbents in their respective parishes more strictly where their duty requires them, would have a better effect infinitely, in improving and reforming the morals of the present age, than a thousand proclamations issued from his Majesty by advice of his privy council, for suppressing vice and immorality, and the superfluous number of houses of public resort, those nurseries of every species of wickedness and villainy.

The proclamation I allude to, was that published about four years ago, and not the late one for preventing the discussion of political subjects, relative to reforming any abuses or defects

defects that may be from length of time required in our excellent constitution, &c. With respect to the former, what has been the consequence? Have the morals of the lower order of people been in any degree amended and improved since that period? Have the number of public houses been lessened? So far otherwise, that it is universally remarked, that they have increased in an *incredible degree*, under the denomination of liquor shops, wine vaults, &c. but in reality are no other than places licensed by trading justices, where the most pernicious liquid poison is vended to the prejudice of the health and morals of both sexes, inflaming and exciting them to every kind of disorder.

With respect to the late proclamation for suppressing the discussion of subjects relative to the management of public affairs, &c. I am apt to fear it will have a very different effect than what is expected; it will tend to excite farther enquiry into the conduct of administration, and the supposed abuses and defects which a lapse of time may have occafioned in the constitution, which may require amending, repairing, or renovating.

The spirit of liberty being once entertained by the people, the more it is attempted to be checked and suppressed, the more it will spread and increase; it resembles the palm tree, which is said to spread and flourish in proportion as it is pressed down.

It is a maxim in philosophy, that the same causes will always produce the same effects: and by history we are instructed to judge of the future consequences of things from what under similar circumstances have happened in past ages; for human nature is the same under different periods of the world, a little allowances being made for variations in modes and fashions. I could produce a variety of instances from history in confirmation of the above reflections, was it proper at this time, when so much dread and apprehension are entertained by the rulers of the state, either for the community itself, or for their own power, and extravagant emoluments.

But

But be that as it may, what I wish to recommend and inculcate, is, the necessity there is for the residence of incumbents of benefices where their duty requires: and as servants of the state with liberal incomes, that they be obliged to pay attention and diligence to season the rising generation, the youth of their respective parishes, who are under their care and guidance, as early as possible, with piety towards God, and respect to magistracy; which would produce the most salutary benefit and advantage to the community in general; for from these the hopes of a reform in succeeding generations are to be expected, which, if well grounded, they may retain during the remainder of their days, and may be a means of reforming others also:

Quo semel est imbuta recens servabit odorem,
Testa diu.

The youth, under their inspection, should be taught and made sensible of the absolute necessity neceffity of paying an uniform and unqualified obedience to the laws of the gofpel, in oppofition to the diforderly propenfities of fenfe, and the immoral maxims of the world; this is an employment for which the feveral incumbents of parifhes are amply paid; this they have folemnly engaged at their inftitution to perform *perfonally*, and not by proxy, &c. but which is too frequently neglected, as matters beneath their dignity in general, and fit only for their fubftitutes to attend to. But thefe lofty gentlemen do not reflect, that fuch an employ would by no means difparage them, however exalted they may be as minifters of the gofpel; as it is 'no other than co-operating with the benevolent author of the univerfe, when they endeavour to train up free and intelligent beings to fuch a degree of moral perfection, as may fit and prepare them for eternal happinefs in a future ftate, which their duty requires.

As fervants of the ftate, it is more immediately the bufinefs of the clergy to do every thing in their power to promote the peace and good

good order of the community, by endeavouring to throw the controul of piety over the impetuosity of appetite, when they oppose the restraint of religion *over* the seduction of the world; for the tranquility, and indeed the *very existence* of every civil community, is endangered when religion has lost its influence over the minds of its members.

PART THE THIRD.

Treats of that denomination of people, stiled
CURATES.

SINCE then it must be allowed by every intelligent person, that religion contributes so greatly to the advancement of the great ends of government, it would surely be a matter of prudence and policy in the civil magistrate, as well as the great men of the state, of whom our legislators are composed, to protect and encourage such as are professors and teachers of it; and particularly the inferior part of the clergy, upon whom, as before hinted, devolves now nearly the whole care of the souls of the people of the established church of England, the whole administration of religion, as matters are now conducted; since the superior part, whose most *immediate business* it is, have in a manner abandoned them, by their non-residence, as unworthy and beneath their

their concern, it may be averred with strictest truth, that the poor curates at present are the only apostolic clergy of this nation; for they LITERALLY *both hunger and thirst, are naked, are buffeted, and have no certain dwelling-place,* according to St. Paul. And as the clergy of this kingdom* have the greatest intercourse with the people, by frequently conversing with them, they have the chief opportunity of forming their principles, and directing their consciences, as well as disposing and guiding their inclinations and affections. This body of men are free from that supercilious hauteur so disgusting in their dignified brethren, from the nature of their humble condition; also free from that litigious contention for tythes, &c. which lower the beneficed clergy so much in the esteem of their parishioners. They gain the attention of the greatest part of the inhabitants of the whole realm, once every week at least; they have an opportunity of ruling their passions, and tempering their prejudices, &c. Upon this ground then, I am of opinion, that it would be *no bad policy* in government

ment to attach them to its interests as firmly as possible, by the surest ties and motives of affection and gratitude.

Quam plurimis amicitiis fortuna Principis indigat, præcipuum est Principis opus amicos parare.

Plin.

Should any civil commotion ever happen amongst us, which might disturb the state (which may divine Providence ever avert) there is no better expedient than to encourage those who have now the guidance of the people in spiritual concerns, to put them in mind to be subject to *principalities and powers; to submit themselves to every ordinance of man for the Lord's sake; not to speak evil of the ruler of the people; not to curse the king in their hearts; but to obey magistrates, and pray for those who are in authority, that we may live peaceably and quietly under them.* From these subjects they have it in their power to influence their respective congregations to act

act in support of our present happy establishment.

In the present state of things, these poor subalterns in the church, seem to be cut off in a manner from the body of the clergy, to be fallen off from the consideration of the legislature. The meanness of their condition, and the severe oppression they experience from their superiors, dispirit them, and cramp their endeavours for the public good; and what is extraordinary, and extremely discouraging, even in those very statutes which are enacted for *the maintenance of the poor clergy*, the distressed curates are never considered, though so useful a body of people. Every vicar, every *beneficed curate*, that hath something *certain* to depend upon of his own, promises himself some little farther advantage from a royal augmentation, I mean Queen Anne's bounty: but the poor curate hath nothing to depend upon, but to live at the mercy of a haughty, domineering, hard-hearted master, who pays him as he pleases, treats him as he thinks proper, and dismisses him according to his pleasure and caprice. The scripture says, *to him that hath shall be given, and from him that hath not shall be taken away, even that which he hath.*

The only statute law that hath been provided in favour of the curates, as a barrier against their oppressors, has been limited in its bounds, and evaded in its execution.

It is earnestly to be hoped that the legislature, when they come to understand the *real* hardships and oppressions this most useful body of people (I may without exaggeration affirm in the whole nation) labour under, and the infinite benefit that would arise to the whole body of people of the established church, in the improvement of their morals and religious duties, were the inferior clergy put upon a more respectable footing: I say, when this comes to be understood and considered, it is to be hoped, the present heavy yoke will be removed from the necks of these *hewers of wood and drawers of water*, as they are considered by their employers, that they may in some measure be relieved, and their condition bettered, by by the wisdom, sound policy, and humanity of the legislature; that the calumny and reproach of the clergy of the established church being the greatest tyrants to each other, may be removed; and that it may not be said, that the legislature have been more attentive, compassionate, and solicitous to relieve the natives of AFRICA, than they are to relieve their fellow countrymen of the same religion, who are the most aggrieved, distressed, despised part of his Majesty's subjects, on account of their poverty and indigence; at present, they are really become a bye-word; the epithet *poor* is invariably and universally annexed to the appellation of curate.

In the present state of luxury and dissipation in this kingdom, a hair-dresser will acquire more in *one* attendance upon a lady or gentleman, than a clergyman by an attendance at the ALTAR of God; and an Italian musician, or a celebrated female singer, will acquire more by one performance, than a poor curate's salary will amount to for a whole year's duty in the church in the service of God: this is

absolutely

absolutely true, without the least exaggeration.

Matters being in this deplorable situation, it is in vain to attempt to assert and maintain the dignity of profession and station; this would only tend to draw upon them a farther degree of ridicule and contempt; for when the mind is bowed down by distress and penury, it is impossible, by any effort whatever, to bear up against contempt and scorn.

It may be urged by some inconsiderate persons, that these unfortunate oppressed body of men are to blame, in submitting to such scanty salaries allowed them by their illiberal employers: but the misfortune is, the bishops have put it in the power of the beneficed clergy to avail themselves of the ascendancy they have over the poor curates, who, if they express themselves in the least dissatisfied with the salary imposed upon them, are instantly told, that they have several who are ready to engage to perform the duty, upon the same or lower terms; and that they are at liberty to quit as soon as they pleafe, if they do not approve of what is allowed them.

What can a perfon do in this fituation? Notwithftanding he is engaged in a profeffion by which he cannot fupport himfelf, there is no receding; there is no other means of his fubfiftence: he will reflect, that it will be prudent to fubmit to the incompetent allowance he then has, than to be entirely without any engagement.

This is owing to our fpiritual governors the bifhops, as before hinted, ordaining fo many mean wretches, of all defcriptions, without being regularly educated, the lame, the halt, and the almoft blind, illiterate mechanics, &c. which has been the caufe of reducing the moft honourable of all profeffions to fo much contempt.

When a high prieft, endued with a little more liberality than the generality of his beneficed brethren, grants his fubftitute fifty or fixty pounds a year, when a vacancy happens in fo rich a piece of *curatical preferments*; there will be as much emulation to fucceed, and

and application to acquire it, as among our right reverend fathers for the disproportionately endowed see of Durham, which upon an average, *communibus annis*, is valued by some at fifteen thousand pounds a year; but some years, by the falling in and renewing of leases, &c. considerably more. What an enormous disproportion between persons of the same profession! Such a prelate's postillion or porter is much better provided for than a poor curate, although sometimes as well educated, and of superior abilities to his Lordship.

The late bishop of a certain see, was originally a crape weaver at Norwich. There is now a person who is a prebendary and archdeacon, brother to a certain bishop, who has been so rapidly advanced by Mr. Pitt, *who was a little while ago behind a counter*. The curates in the metropolis and large towns must, to avoid contempt, make the best appearance their scanty allowances will admit of, which often occasions very disagreeable embarrassments and difficulties; so that it may be said of them, *Commune id vitium*

vitium est, hic vivimus ambitiosa paupertate, omnes.

Such are the modes of acquiring promotion at present in the church, that a person of mean appearance can have no pretensions, let his merit and long standing in the ministry be what they may, when a person of affluence, connected with men in power, stands in competition against him.

Haud facile emergunt, quorum virtutibus obstat,
Res angusta domi.

I have before hinted, and must inculcate it, that *in general* whatever presents the officiating curate receives above the stated fees, by the generosity or liberality of any of the parishioners, though he is under the necessity of making his obeisance for what is supposed to be for *himself*; yet he is *generally*, under the strictest stipulation, to refund to his employer immediately when the ceremony is performed. There are instances of some unfortunate persons

sons in the humiliating situation of curates, who by the duty they perform in the church, do not acquire even the interest of the money expended upon their education, which is a most melancholy truth.

Is this a sufficient recompence for all the anxious care and thought that the good old father has been at, in endeavouring to promote the welfare and advancement of his son in the world? Is this an equivalent for the fatigue of a long studious application?

Must a man for this be accomplished in every branch of literature, and particularly of divinity and oratory? How much wiser in point of prudence, as things are at present conducted in the church, would that parent be, who disposes of his son in some mechanical business, than to a profession in which, without friends or means of purchasing preferment, he must probably be a beggar for the mere honor of being styled a gentleman, which is the case with a great part of the clergy of the established church.

The

The clergy of the church of Rome have, it is true, in many places, no confiderable allowance. But what may not a man acquire who is fuppofed to be a retainer of an infallible head, the maker of a God in every confecration of the hoft? What may not he extract from the pockets of the people by auricular confeffion, forgiving fins, freeing fouls from purgatory, admitting fouls into heaven; befides a great variety of more profitable tales, cheats, and lying wonders under his management and adminiftration?

Diffenting teachers of every denomination have ample provifion made for them, by fubfcriptions, rents of pews, collections frequently under various pretences, &c. and particularly methodift preachers, who now are become fo numerous in every part of the kingdom; who commence fuch without the leaft knowledge or application to ftudy, illiterate mechanicks who have nothing to recommend them befides an hypocritical demeanour and appearance, a *pretence to infpiration*; yet thefe are the perfons who ftyle themfelves, by way of eminence,

eminence and distinction, *gospel ministers*. These have the address to extract from the pockets of their ignorant, infatuated, enthusiastic followers a most comfortable revenue and plentiful maintenance, *devouring widows houses, and for a pretence making long prayer.*

The most mortifying and humiliating circumstances of all to the poor curates, particularly in the metropolis, is their being lorded over, and treated with familiarity and contempt by the parish clerks, on account of the superiority of their incomes from the church, to the salaries of the curates.

But to carry the matter into some of its serious consequences—How can it otherwise be, but that contempt and poverty must be the effect of such incompetent allowance? It is in vain to attempt correcting the opinion of mankind, even the wiser part will follow the vulgar, in esteeming men according to their wealth, dignities, and honors; few have such logical heads to be able to distinguish the man from his profession, and reverence him as a divine, while they despise him on account of his

his poverty. The vulgar especially cannot suppose that a spectre of a man, labouring under distress, can preach as powerfully, and petition heaven as prevalently, as the dignitary pluralist who appears in pomp and splendor. The wise man of Sirach has more gravely remarked this difference: When the rich man speaketh, says he, every one holdeth his peace, and his words are extolled to the clouds; but, if a poor man speaketh, they are ready to say, what fellow is this? Agreeable to this the French poet Boileau says,

La richesse permet une juste fierté !
Mais il faut être souple avec la pauvreté.

From the several calculations in political arithmetic, that have been made by Doctor Price and others, the inhabitants of this kingdom, allowing six to a house, may amount to about seven millions. Out of this number let us suppose two millions to be Roman catholics, Jews, and Dissenters of every denomination, there will then be five millions of souls who

who fall under the care of the clergy of the established church, I mean the inferior clergy, the curates, whose distresses render them so contemptible in the eyes of the laity in general, that their administration is not attended with that weight it otherwise would have.

The poverty of the first preachers of the gospel in the primitive times of Christianity was so far from being despicable, that it was rather honourable, as performing their duty from conscientious motives; but in these times of luxury and dissipation, and refinement of manners, nothing appears more disgraceful and contemptible than a garb that favours of penury. Every person now is esteemed in proportion to the figure he makes in the world, *fas aut nefas*, no matter which way the means of supporting it is acquired.

It was exactly the same in the degenerate time of the Romans, when the proconsuls, like our *nabobs*, as they are styled, returned home laden with the spoils of the provinces of the East. It was customary for their friends to write to them not to return to Rome till they had

had acquired sufficient wealth to be able to bribe the senate. We have seen something resembling this in our times. Luxury and profligacy of manners among them, had arrived to such a pitch, that worth and merit became of no estimation, were laughed totally out of countenance. According to Juvenal's observation, who lived at that time,

Et genus et virtus, nisi cum re, est vilior algâ.
Juv.

Had a curate of thirty or forty pounds a year salary, labouring under indigence and poverty, the united eloquence of the two celebrated orators of Greece and Rome, Demosthenes and Cicero, as well as the learning of all our able divines who have wrote so very excellently upon theological subjects, yet their doctrine will be received with coolness and indifference, will have no effect, nor make the least impression upon the generality, who judge more by appearance than reality. In a word, in the present age of luxury and frivolity, poverty is
the

the moſt mortifying diſgrace that can befal a man.

Poverty, in the opinion of ſome, is ſtyled a kind of hell upon earth; and he who labours under this misfortune, anticipates, in ſome degree, the torments of the unhappy in a future ſtate. It eclipſes the brighteſt virtues, is the ſepulchre of great and noble deſigns, deprives a man of genius of the means of accompliſhing what nature fitted him for, ſtifling the moſt laudable purpoſes in their embryo. How many illuſtrious ſouls may be ſaid to have been dead, in a manner, among the living, or buried alive in the obſcurity of their condition, whoſe talents and capacities would have rendered them the brighteſt ornaments of their country! yet the inſuperable penury of their conditions has ranked them among the outcaſts of the earth in the ſight of men.

The preſent ſtate of this kingdom reſembles in a great degree that of ancient Rome, as before hinted, when an inundation of wealth had corrupted the manners of its citizens, the

power

power of fashion became superior to that of law.

MORES LEGES PERDUXERUNT IN POTES-
TATEM SUAM.

If an angel from heaven, I believe, should descend amongst us, and take upon him the ministerial function, if he abstained from working miracles, under the same discouragements and difficulties that the present curates of the established church, he would acquire not much respect to his person, or attention to his doctrine.

There are no denominations of men in the kingdom, clerks in public offices under government, common excisemen, mechanics of every kind, &c. who have not applied for an advancement of their salaries and wages, in consequence of the high price of provisions, and every necessary of life, difference in the value of money, as well as alteration in the manner of living amongst us; even journeymen taylors have had their wages settled by act of Parliament, at a higher rate than the curates in general are allowed by their rectors for officiating in the service of the church. Even the negroes of Africa have had the *omnipotent* minister of the present day, and the first orators in the house of Commons, for their advocates, to relieve them from the tyranny of their hard task-masters. The distressed desponding curates are the *only set of men* in the realm, who are neglected, and whose salaries have not been advanced, and that bear no kind of proportion with the revenues of their employers, whose benefices have been greatly advanced, as before hinted; but that the salaries of the curates continue the same at this time as settled near a hundred years ago. The last act of Parliament for the regulation of curates was in the former part of the reign of Queen Anne, when it was enacted, that they were to receive no less than 20*l.* nor more than 50*l.* a year, the proportioning which was left to the ordinary; but if the curate had not a licence, he could not avail himself of *even* this pittance.

It is universally allowed, that the contempt that

that useful body of men, the curates, are held in on account of their poverty, is one of the chief causes of the desertion from the established church, the rapid and alarming increase of all kinds of sectaries, particularly of that of methodism, which is inconceivable, through every part of the kingdom; and yet these oppressed indigent people are the persons upon whom *now* the care of the greater part of the souls of the members of the established church are devolved.

Some persons have maintained, that the state of the clergy is the best means of judging of a people of any nation.

The present earl of Guildford, when a member of the house of Commons, speaking of Mr. Beaufoy's Bill in favour of the Dissenters, declared it as his decided opinion, that the situation of the established church was the criterion by which the world measure the flourishing state of the constitution. If this position be true, then such as are acquainted with the many abuses subsisting in our church, and the extraordinary desertion from it in consequence of them, muft form a very indifferent opinion *indeed* of our conftitution.

Exclufive of the benefits which may be expected from the improved ftate of religion in this kingdom, confidered in a fpiritual fenfe, I mean refpecting the happinefs and rewards to be expected in a future ftate; yet in a political view our fecular governors well know, that the beft and fureft foundation of their authority over mankind is laid in RELIGION; that human laws, and the terrors of them, can only bind the outward man; but confcience, which is the inward man, can by no other means be bound than by the ties of RELIGION, and the rewards and punifhments of a future ftate. For this reafon, fome of the wifeft heathens have ever efteemed it more expedient to humour the vulgar in their miftakes relative to a future ftate (becaufe how grofs foever they appeared to be, they found them ferviceable to keep them in fubjection), rather than endanger the government by invalidating their belief. For the fame reafon, even atheiftical politicians advife their princes, in all ages, to take efpecial

cial care of religion, and to see it rooted as firmly as possible in the hearts of their subjects, and held in veneration, respect, and esteem; how little soever they might *inwardly* regard it themselves; because it is the only instrument of government, and the most effectual expedient of maintaining their subjects under controul.

So shamefully inadequate is the stipend allowed the curates amongst us, that it is a notorious truth, that an eminent barrister at law will gain more by one particular cause of importance, than a curate's salary would amount to in *seven years*. When the late Lord Grantley, or better known perhaps by the title of Sir Fletcher Norton, attended at the bar, being the first person who received these extravagant sums, it was not uncommon for him to receive two or three hundred guineas as a retaining fee. Lord Ashburton, the late Mr. Dunning, followed his example by exacting the same immoderate sums; by which *practices* they both amassed greater fortunes than the whole collective body of curates in the nation are

are capable of doing during their lives; notwithstanding many of them are better educated and of superior abilities, though not of equal *effrontery* with the two gentlemen above mentioned.

With the highest elevation of fifty pounds a year, as settled by the legislature near a hundred years ago, which was then equal to three times that sum, *at least at present*, a gentleman (for such the curates must be styled) notwithstanding their distressed condition, and that journeymen mechanicks, who have better incomes, burlesque them upon that account: I say, a person will find it difficult to live and appear in any degree as a gentleman, when the high price of provisions, and every article of life, as well as the present mode of living, are considered: and he will be an extraordinary œconomist indeed, if at the expiration of the year, he finds not himself *minus*, in the language of the algebraists; but, upon supposition that he has a wife and some olive branches around his table, what a distressed state must he then be in! perpetually struggling to free himself

self from the embarrassments of debt, and as perpetually relapsing. What a primitive sight in these days of dissipation, luxury, and universal foppery, to se a *man of God* traversing the streets of this gay metropolis in his threadbare coat, for spruce powdered shopmen and apprentices to point at, and wags to crack their jokes upon.

To be serious, how is it possible to conceive, that a man obliged to appear under the character of a gentleman, can subsist upon such a pittance, I do not say with decency, but *in any degree*, without being plunged into difficulties, and reduced to the necessity of crouching and stooping to such debasing actions, as must render both himself and his administration contemptible, and such as his soul would spurn at under other circumstances. Were he indeed in any expectation of arriving at preferment, after such a course of starving and extreme distress and mortification, he probably might strive to bear up against these difficulties with patience and magnanimity.

The

The only recourse a poor curate has of improving his income, as his family increases, and his exigencies require, is commencing pedagogue, engaging in the business of educating youth, the most disagreeable of all the employs of life. A melancholy reflection after so much expence, time, and study, which, if employed in any secular business or occupation, might have enabled him to live comfortably in plenty, and perhaps acquire a fortune against the decline of life, and provision for his children, who, as matters are at present, are generally under the management of trustees of charitable societies, &c.

In the metropolis and large towns, a curate endeavours to make a little addition to his income, by entering the lists for a lectureship; to acquire which, such mean debasing arts are used, such prostitution of character, such defamation, reviling, such envious emulation, &c. are practised, as are a disgrace to religion, and the clerical profession; and if he who will not cringe and fawn upon the meanest of the people,

people, can expect no success in his pulpit prize-fighting. St. Paul makes mention of some in his days, who preached Christ for *envy, strife*, and *contention*; what we see in our times is somewhat similar to this.

Such as are engaged in secular affairs, in case of accident, sickness, inability, through age, &c. such as are free of any of the companies in trade in London, or most of the large towns in the kingdom, have all a comfortable retreat and maintenance in the decline of life: but the *man of God*, who hath dedicated his life in the service of the altar, hath not, under the above distress, *where to lay his head*.

There have been two recent instances of clergymen dying, as supposed, for want of necessary sustenance; one was in Bartholomew hospital, the other was in Wiltshire: but how many are there *who cannot dig, but to beg are ashamed*, who pine in obscurity, whose cases are not so publickly known.

The bishop of Landaff's advice to the society of curates, who applied to him lately for his Lordship's advice respecting an application

tion to parliament for a redress of their grievances, was to this effect; that if the legislature does not take their miserable unhappy situation into consideration, with that of their brethren through the rest of the kingdom, and if no relief is to be expected; "that they must look forward with CONTENT to that awful day, when all superiority shall be done away, except superior goodness, and no degree of merit fail of its reward:" it is extremely *easy* for a person in affluent circumstances to give such advice; but it is very *difficult* for such as have been delicately and liberally educated, and who once have enjoyed probably the conveniences and comforts of life plentifully, and with prospects of living independently in the world, to sit down CONTENTED under the combined misfortune of suffering hunger, popression, as well as contempt, scorn, and derision, and all *this for righteousness sake*; having for many years, in the prime of their lives, performed their duty with faithfulness and diligence in their profession, for perhaps an ungrateful, illiberal, opulent pluralist.

His

His Lordship gave it as his opinion at the same time, that the incumbents of benefices were as much diftreffed as the curates. But with due deference to his Lordship, I muft fay, that this is a very great error indeed.

The benefices that have occafion for curates are fuch as belong to non-refident pluralifts, which have been, as above ftated, greatly improved by inclofures of Common Fields, and tythes advanced twice or three times over, without any advance perhaps to the perfon who performs the whole of the duty. A rectory I held for fome years before an inclofure took place, amounted to no more than a hundred and twenty pounds a year, which at this time is above two hundred and fifty pounds. There has been a very great advance through the whole kingdom wherever there are great tythes, that is, in the rectories. Even the condition of all the inferior incumbents, the vicars, is greatly preferable to that of the curates. Suppofe a perfon is incumbent of a fmall vicarage, he faves the expence of houferent, has a garden, orchard, and generally a little glebe to supply a horse, and a cow or two, besides some small endowment; something arising annually from Easter offerings, surplice fees and presents, an opportunity of improving his little glebe, which may now be of something more value, since the decision relative to aggistment tythes. Whereas the miserable curate must rent a house or lodging for himself and family, enjoys none of the above conveniences and advantages, has nothing besides his bare 30*l.* or 40*l.* a year, the average of the salary allowed to furnish every article for himself and family, which at these times is a very scanty support indeed.

I have been thus particular in contrasting the condition of the smallest benefice with that of a curate, to convince his Lordship of the many advantages the *former* has over the *latter*; besides, another consideration extremely mortifying to a man of spirit and of liberal ideas, the incumbent is for life and independent; whereas he who serves a curacy has a superior to please, by whose caprice he is liable to be dismissed at a short notice; his condition and

and tenure is precarious; but the possessor of the most inconsiderable benefice is independent, and his state is permanent; and what is no less galling, the person who officiates in the capacity of curate, is, by the generality of the laity (particularly the vulgar part) considered as acting in a state of servitude, and is treated accordingly.

The *Levites* in the *Old Testament* had plentiful provisions: they had houses, glebe-lands, free-will-offerings, and their part of the first fruits and sacrifices. Do the inferior Ministers of the Gospel, the Curates, deserve worse wages, for bringing better tidings? Besides the *Levite*'s office was hereditary, and the son was sure of succeeding his father in his house and lands, with a faculty *ad succedendum Patri*.

With respect to improving himself in the knowledge requisite for the better discharge of his function, the poor Curate is totally precluded, having it not in his power to furnish himself with such books as are necessary for that purpose; and if he had, the anxiety of his mind under the pressure of his indigent circumstances,

stances, prevents him from paying due attention to his studies. A mind at ease is absolutely requisite for study, and the acquisition of any science, when a man is embarrassed in his affairs under misfortunes, he drags perpetually about him a heavy chain, which in every effort he makes, weighs down his fancy, and enervates his style. If the curates, from the narrowness of their incomes, are not in a capacity of furnishing themselves with such books as are necessary, they cannot maintain the honour and well-being of the church, they cannot defend the cause of Christianity in general, or the reformed religion in particular, as they ought to do; should they be found deficient, it is not to be wondered at. It is from the wealthy pluralists and dignitaries, who have the means of purchasing, and the leisure of studying books, that we must expect the advancement of sciences, the understanding of mysteries, the explication of obscure passages, the resolving of difficult cases, the stating of controversies, confutation of errors, and, in fine, the confirmation of all truth.

What a daily triumph muſt it be to the infidels of the age, that the very men who have the buſineſs of inſtructing nearly the whole of the people of England (I mean of the eſtabliſhed church) in the principles of religion, ſhould not be able, on account of the above ſtated diſcouragements, to ſupport them by ſound argument, and be able to demonſtrate the divine authority of that bleſſed book from whence they daily preach.

What I wiſh to inculcate in general, is, that contempt muſt be the unavoidable effect of ſo incompetent a proviſion as falls to the lot of the ſubſtitutes who perform nearly the whole of the duty in the eſtabliſhed church amongſt us: and it is impoſſible to correct the opinions of mankind; even the wiſer part will follow the vulgar, in eſteeming men according to their wealth, dignities, and honours, notwithſtanding the abſurdity of the thing, conſidered in a rational light. And though the reſpect that is due, is ſettled, as has been already ſhewn, upon a clergyman on account of his ſacerdotal character, and in that reſpect is unalterable by

any

any circumstance of fortune; yet few people have such logical heads as to be able to distinguish, or such nice conceptions as to separate the man from his profession, and so reverence him as a divine, while they despise him on account of his poverty: few persons have such unprejudiced minds, as not to esteem an ecclesiastic in proportion to the value of his preferment, and suppose that he rises and falls in his pulpit abilities, according to the glare and splendid appearance that accompanies him.

When the pompous pluralist visits his parishioners to receive his revenue for glebe tythe, &c. he will condescend to give them a sermon, as before hinted: upon return home after service, upon being asked who preached, the ladies *particularly* will answer in raptures, that the doctor *himself* had given them a *charming* discourse; but the great man having settled for his dues, taken his departure, and left the care of his flock to the hireling, who sometimes is a man of superior abilities and the better orator, there are no further *charming* discourses.

I could

I could enumerate a variety of other abuses which subsist in the established church of this kingdom; but shall conclude at present by earnestly wishing, that the rulers of the state, among other laws for the benefit of the community, would deign to look into the *sanctuary* also, and see whether some better regulations may not be wanting there; lest some provocations of divine wrath may not proceed from thence: for if the complaint of those *who reap down the field*, or any other hirelings, *defrauded of their just wages*, enters the ears of the Almighty; what will not the oppression of his more *immediate* servants do? *Woe to him that coveteth an evil covetousness to his house*, and detaineth from his poor hireling curate an *equitable* and *proportionate recompence* for his labour and duty in the vineyard.

FINIS.